VISHUDDHA

VISHUDDHA

by Ian Cook

Anamcara Press LLC

Published in 2024 by Anamcara Press LLC

Author © 2024 Ian Cook
Book design by Maureen Carroll
Georgia, Timeburner, and Minion Pro.
Printed in the United States of America.

Book Description: Unlock the self through verse. Ian Cook's poetic odyssey traces silence to speech, forging connection through language, sound, and symbols. A journey of growth, mental health, and resonating authenticity.

ANAMCARA PRESS LLC
P.O. Box 442072, Lawrence, KS 66044
https://anamcara-press.com/

Ordering Information:
Quantity sales. Special discounts are available on quantity purchases by corporations, associations, and others. For details, contact the publisher at the address above.
Orders by U.S. trade bookstores and wholesalers. Please contact Ingram Distribution.

Cook, Ian, Author
Vishuddha

POE005060 - POETRY / American / Asian American & Pacific Islander
POE023010   POETRY / Subjects & Themes / Death, Grief.
SEL040000 - SELF-HELP / Communication & Social Skills
SEL009000 - SELF-HELP / Creativity

ISBN-13: 978-1-960462-31-2 (Paperback)
ISBN-13: 978-1-960462-32-9 (Hardcover)
ISBN-13: 978-1-960462-33-6 (EBook)

Library of Congress Control Number: 2023951566

*"If what I say resonates with you,
it is merely because we are both branches
on the same tree."*

—W.B. Yeats

Contents

PART I: What I tried to say but had to sing first

PART II: The Lonesome Night flowering forth Morning Light

PART III: Sacred Places

PART IV: Trepidations

PART V: Family Matters

PART VI: Apparition and Old Ghost

DEDICATION—

To my sister Fiona, for showing me the way. I hope you've found your way too, wherever you are. I love you, I miss you.

VISHUDDHA

what does communication mean to me an opening of the mouth
making shapes and letting sound out to learn to speak, have my
self be spoken, and it be heard and understood that is the path,
through space and ether realizing the godself and making it
known never center but always the middle by the brain and the
heart and the body making waves with waves, expressing what is
ethereal and letting that vibrate throughout ALL reality shaped
by a series of words said by a thing made of reality manifesting
intention at the speed of speaking

PART I:
What I tried to say but had to sing first

Hermes (Petasos)

Old friend, my pen sings to you, spills ink for you,
in the curves and quick cuts of my letters,
connected in cursive flowing, inscribing my well
intentions, for myself and those around me, for
what will be, should be, manifested sweetly
in the waking day of life. I carve a home for wishes
to sit upon the page, and hope for them to come true,
in time, as all good things do, in time.
I spell, make spells, cast magic, become magical.
If this way of words can be taught to others, I
have honored you – spread your name across space and
time and I too am transported thus.
Thank you for the tune upon which my tongue dances,
this heavenly song sings ringing across
the cathedral of my mind, carving out new corridors
for the vibrations to resonate within, and
then out into the rest of my being. In steady words
upon the page, I commune with you,
communicate through you, and carry you
with me always.

Ian Cook

Murmuration

stark, talon'd, invasive
a habit of hard flight
direct headed, gregarious

borrowed speech
pattern of alarm
Starling shows how to listen

lilting neighbor followed; following
a cloud; chattering congregation clattering

Atramentous

I should have written love letters all along
loath to leave
instead, spelling out what was not wanted in silence.
and so I lost my voice —
content to seek
an accuracy, I would want
to speak
or at least understand
within myself

an outline around my form where there should be none
and I am the blank page babbled upon
scrawl rewritten in name of what I have not done
I am the last drop of ink spread thin and desperate.

what were those words that I tried to remember?
the Lexis muttered upon my tongue turns it heavy
It struck hard – a violent chord within my throat.
It made me; it sounded me out like the vowels of a howl.

Golden Grove

old oil lamp light smolders slow
to keep warmth inclusive of the lonely night
morning hours are bided in time
when the Day-Dog doubles over in holler
the sunrise is a taut lie
supplied upon Old Sky to make fire

what is the present when it is always becoming the past?

a stone skipping down the well and all left is broad
stroked echo
never breathing in the moment
by no means here
or now
but recounting past selves down in the deep divide;
what was action and what was mistake
when
retrospection upsets, there is fault to be unearthed
and it was all yours
glorified and shorn
to make room for more

we are told it is all for naught

A Skeleton Come Alive

i am just bones
page wrapped
scratched patchwork
paper thick
pitch ink
tongue speaking tongues
dipped quill tip deep; leaving a void
invade the soft parts of fingers, a long spine
like the summer sun in the iris,
or hand placed firm,
a matted mane lay long in the lost crevice
between shoulder blades.

voices wisp; curled to hide in deep sung verses
from Mouth making new shapes.

Collapses

People look ugly when they cry
taking the moment to look in the mirror
and reaffirm the fact — we were born hideous
silently making love, watching whispering fingers
on your lip, somatic Braille spelling
"now can you see"

Cassandra roped to the rocks
she, assaulted by snakes licking ears clean
eyes sown open because someone doesn't know
how to talk to girls
she will see the world's end as it comes
out from her mouth, chaotic, and into
the endless wonder of
"no, you are the liar"

A need to be violent
when mongrel switch flips and we are hunched, lurching,
it comes quick like winter winds before
the leaves start to die, like the Blue Jay becomes terror
amongst emerald prisons, wardens of the wild brush,
whistling through a barely open beak
"which voice should we listen to"

Waking with the moon in the noonday glow,
it clears a path through dust and celestial dynasty
counting senescent stars that needed to be named
finding the oldest; I lent the last name given to me
and knew it would suffice
as it collapsed upon itself.

L'appel Du Vide

I lit a cigarette at the wrong end and smoked it halfway
stubbed dead ash upon palms
to smear long letters on a wall
unafraid of wayward winds and letting go, of change
tending noticed glances and half smiles, set loose
made sure they were counted for
board up in the whole silence of sacred solitude
nourished, licking fingers slogged with ink
spitting up unhurried cursive in the exhale
in the frail consciousness of waking breath
the length of the larynx distends
the wind bending the sigh
exhaling a ghost
still husk

when I die I'll be closer to god because I won't   exist

Ian Cook

Doggerel

here is strewn tangle:

to tell what words mean to me
scale placed with tender touch
or haphazard hand to make sure of balance
right, regardless
give speculation – be prosperous
cash in rhymes to buy more vowels

cast about, jumping ship to get the bends out
shake the host to leave a ghost in place

strip the bone to bodhi
breath in tandem with the trees

benefit from vibration
absorb denotation
sketch the unlit corner sitting dim
in the back of unfettered thought
stretch ink thin to get every last uncertainty out
make the body something of value
so I can waste myself in petty spending
change-handing to wordless and wanting
until I stand empty handed

Haemato

first breath like the smoke of fire from newspaper clips
and bad bibles
a "thank you" read in short hand
simple sanguine notes of re-steps crawled up
through my spine;
we ask for reasons for time spent sifting sand
through a convex hourglass
The Ocean says
i am right
how the waves sway back and forth
it begs
i tried
soft as night, broken in two
widow fights for some sign of time
days off the calendar,
months, aren't quite as accurate
to remember, like lines of conversation
mumbled quiet in desperation
sing of a cold autumn afternoon,
Sparrows flight seemed much too soon
uncertain what these hands should do,
idle by and forget what's new
bloodletting to bear the spirit
glance last like reflections in mirrors
that look away as you open your eyes
time and tide stretch like hands that reach down and
through my veins.

Sundial

The self:
(a) empty space at a center of a star
(b) distance from limb end to end
(c) soul sliver; remains in sonorous sleep

dismissed notice
fragmentary variance cast across cosma
familiar final fate
infinite distance between insides
expands the edge of empty
meets open all; an assemblage of hawks holler

further existence upon ever-vista, tilted universe
fast pulling undiscovered way
impulse of emotion ephemeral
thousand-fold flowering; wringing memory
colossal — completely conscious
absence is all we can affirm
sad self's silent passing
fear and hope bellow, a low murmur
bended tree recovers from the heavy wind
when we cease to be — become more, then we were once
word-spoken to carry the weight of the world
my mother is the flame lighting the end of existence

The Bellicose

Pay no attention to the man behind the curtain

a machination of things to be forgotten
a past self; conscious future, stock
a mottled mask made for daily wear
a host to test the metal
broad strokes on tin
with a full arm
with a haggard pace
with a chest huffed
with king cowardice
with a mind full
grant solid wishes

Bear no resemblance to who used to live in a flat and
settled land

Ian Cook

Black Teeth

sipping ink, staring coarse, locusts bloom at slow noon,
sundown, blissful content, what wants
worries what a sorry waste what bad fate those black
teeth that sorrow that grief.

PART II:
The Lonesome Night flowering forth Morning Light

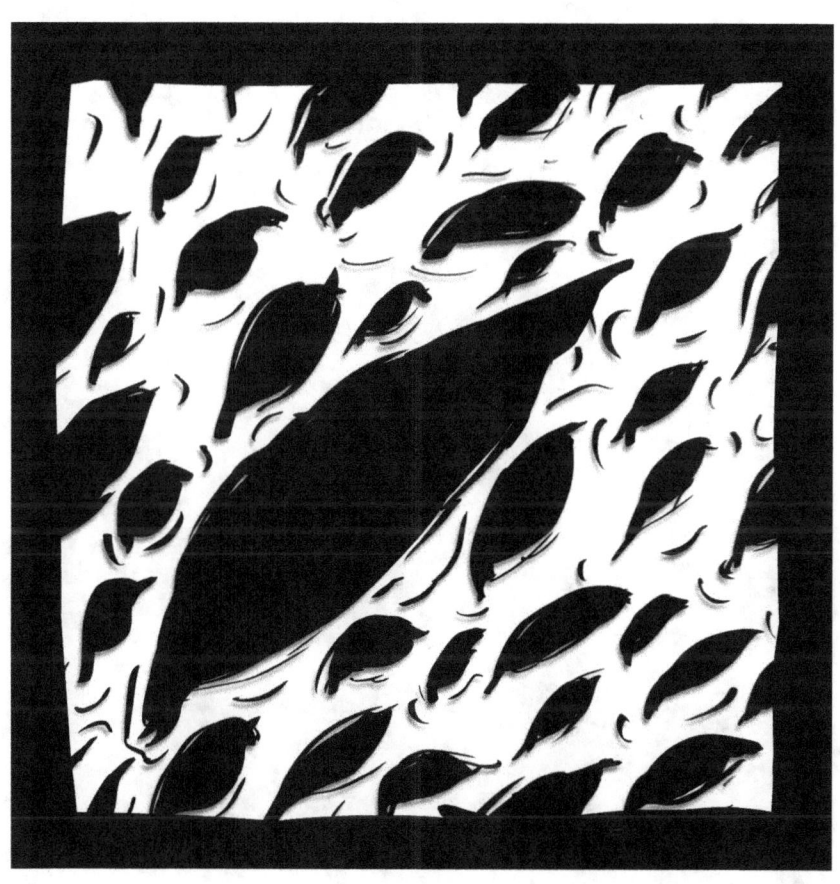

Selamat Malam

Knowing places in the dark
it's alright to wander, sip on sand

in the bottomless palm of Morpheus

Dream Sneak despondent on the plain of deep sleep,
waking up at three o' clock most nights
sheet ice pushes up skin,
symptoms of dust humming low beneath the eye lid
pulling chains of silent slumber,
they hoist the sail fighting against
the breath of quiescence

Medicine Made

I watched fingernails grow
long overnight
a lotus flowering forth from firm fist
to plane palm
porcelain, piercing and invasive

stuck in the lower throat – until drowned
hollow chest hums numb
medicine made electricity dance amid veins
death gripping broken clasps that control hands

Hoarder

let out like lakes, like worldly tendrils wanting,
to question and wither upon the tethered centers
from which they are guided, alongside lines, let alone
when the water divides, who spoke of the holy ghost,
wanting more than a hollow vessel, substantiate,
supplement, draw breath heavy and
never let it out in the blue night, collected in greenhouse
glass, viridian mason jars, kept in case of fires to fan out,
and in the last day's wane it isn't hopeless anymore, body
wrought nerves and thick sinew, stand firm footed,
leaning against the verdant gale.

Ian Cook

Deep Sleep

Drowsing is a waking dream
world wistful in form and place
wishful wondering black existence
for all of after-sundown is hasty caesura

walkabout
in the night
in long leaps
time lies sweet
unbeknownst passage

Death is just a deep sleep
the waking world not yet familiar
dreams are just future states
that set in deja vu manifested

Umbra

it's not the way I was supposed to die
blacked out in the night
knives for eyes
bark blood in my throat
speaking on all fours
knuckle dragger noise, asking to take
from broken hands
from a maw mistakenly maimed
a say-so dismantled like a home
brick from brick and bone for bone

it's not that I don't know you
it's that I never will

Animal body

born in blood
raised in wolves
morning mawl
long borrowed
language bottled
adiabatic embrace
make believe better
biting through thick lip

I love you clearly, in the night
wanting a word for looking away

Lacklove

Bided time is sweet when wasted
waiting up in the night for you
stopped at the bend in the moon
playing catch up across its vista
until I become restless with it —
and beg to borrow your touch

I plan to stay until a solstice wanes
          then follow the fickle wind

Ian Cook

Night Terror

My mother sings still,
as she sleeps within the sun,
I glimpse and go blind.

My father will wail,
howling about tomorrow,
tearing at his throat.

A still spectacle,
black curious wings quick clipped,
flightless without sight.

Lain light, half shadows,
swallow wallows home sallow,
soft morning glow looms.

Darkness deafening
eyesight mired making shapes
naught in the silence

Hollow birch blooms out
towards the loon moon setting
against her psalm skin

Dying on day birthed
void humming, sung all winter
quickness of deep sleep

A Macula

Nothing seems to hold on
in the dead of night
Alone to glean a sold psalm
Keeping time with lies
Breaking bones in the flight
Without a guiding star
Blind surprise
the sun is high
in the Black Soot Sky

If I'm pale and frail so be it
If I'm not a ghost I need some sort of proof

I stood on heels, over the edge of an easy ledge
and was swayed by the motion of the earth
fell forward into dying knoll; left lonely
in uneasy summer.

Ian Cook

Friday, 7:20 AM

I walk with wet steps
Soil sopped treads,
wondering how god
chooses who house-sits

Black Crow bows low in the briar
Wild Vine round and round
White Dogwood bloom,
 sing with the rain.

PART III:
Sacred Places

Straight to Sunrise

The wind through Holy Mountain – a hymn whistling
through the bend in the pine.
They dreamt of a road that reaches into the world,
they'll tear at its heart.
Set upon subterranean holler and wait for echoes to end.
Soot sits black beneath the nail,
and if the earth closes its maw, they'll claw their way out,
leaving names carved in dead ends.

"I've got the blues and the blues got me"

Hark!
Hollows
smoke billows dirty

exhaling a deep breath
straight to sunrise
counting dreams in the well.

Ian Cook

Grandfather Night

The sun a severed neck
Grandfather Night upon the quick vista of
impulsive winter in the languid plains of west Kansas
Incomprehensible fickle haze
Leaped on, lone and ghostly
A foreign incantation crowns tomorrow's rolling morning
Blooming soon
Weeping prayer skips, ringing across open vortex,
the cathedral
Without walls
Passing slow – through still air
Sweet prairie blues led tender along outward gasps
amongst endless air
Soon to hoist hopes in new boon
Doomly moon lofts along the horizon
as a cresting closed eye
Thoughtless until next sun's rise

A Solstice

tawny cast patterns frame
trees as long whispers
with the clouds
sharing secrets of sparrows
bright leafed sycamore
yawns heavy in the wind, tapping
tapping branches, seek,
reach into a window to speak soft
riddles through the bark
led in a maze of splinters
and grooves
we choose
to be lost, following
sweet voices that call us
"brother, sister, child"

Ian Cook

Birds At Night

climb from root to fence to roof
cull quick with a craned nape
bottom beak reaching down
sing more softly in the quiet dark
the low wind is a collective call
furtive and found in the wrong bough

build another nest for the sun
to pass the time besides hunting late
neck cricked to the side in game
two talon around the branch that holds tomorrow's home
glide in sightless to the black and the back porch that
leads to the ravine and the river

Black Breath

Wolf's teeth instead of my own
and I can taste the last words it spoke

I fill pockets with stone and wade into the river
wait for the current to take me to forest
to become lost in the arms of wild wood

demanding my rights of an old elm,
possession of skin that moves makes me king,
and it at once becomes bare branched
and the air becomes poison

but my grizzle gut holds spirits from last winter
ones white with the snow
blind and invisible
the horizon continued into the sky
and there was no need for words like "where"

Bone Tree

standing at the ends of branches and
falling feet first from the Bone Tree
bringing down the clouds
plucking the moon's thin grinned curve
pulling the corners of the night sky
to fashion a new hide
lucid and everywhere
until I become that grand vista
forever stretching my arms out
moving everything further apart
defining an edge of existence for the dead to walk upon
in the hopes that they'll leave me alone
and maybe then I'll enjoy the quiet

Gathering sticks behind grandmother's house
to kindle my pyre

Little Luna

what does it mean
when it's cold only in my room,
dead flies in the middle of January,
a mouth's only moan,
veins mark a map

still a little lost

Ian Cook

Say Something Wonderful,
Say Something Horrible

Out where the trees touch the top of the sky
a stuttered gasp is shared between you and I
it fills chest and we deep breathe because they tell us
it's good
content with land razed, soot and decay.

Out where waves fall off the end of the ocean
A common word was shared between you and I
flowed out through tongues and consumed heart
and mind
wish on a fallen eyelash that floats the current of exhale.

Out where the wind runs out its lungs
a senseless grasp is shared between you and I
It won't fulfill bones, it saps and moans
the soul
fragile patterns mocking hands turning cold.

Who sings to me out in the plains

a grand twisted stranger bending in time
with the wind, jagged gnashing, grind, thistle
silver edged glass rings sway
in time
mingle together
silo singing, hollowed obeisance against the gale
soft wail tip toeing on the tail of a sigh
little whisper, a resonance, leaping low noise
perhaps mourning mother
perhaps lost love
a whistle in the wind
a wind withering wounds

To be a Defeater

I wish I had breathed at the start of the flat sea endeavor,
upon the steady ending ocean and
waited for the fall of the horizon

what would we expect
an edge to stop upon
lean over and let stones fall
for the resounding of the bottomed out deep

hug waters, go over the edge
find the southern
side of existence
explore underneath
meet mirrored selves – their own sun
enamored by old bravery
sails striding new air

written down as fable and then history
for the rest of man joined fain
stories of angels, above

new cities stood with names
ought amongst for last land

Xibalba

we climb roots for limbs
sticking fingers deep into blackened bark,
pull out sticky sweet
tasting thick nectar as we share a staggered breath
carved steps from stone, each taller
regardless of even footholds, even progress
through
and thoroughly
there with me
a long way up
fingers chapped, white dry, snapping
my love ties double knots around her waist
a picture of a meek word spoken
as if rhymed with anything
teeth become sharpened on rocks; they grate together
sing a song written in two parts
croaking chord
like a willow sprouting full grown into a cold night
in May arms become branches
feeling the ground for warmth
green grass

Ian Cook

Plague Abandonment

staid upon a precipice, an abyss
overlooking
peaceable and meek motioned
cloven hoof footed
whatever willed
the fill of sitting still
feet planted deep
making some way

vagabonding sneak
only come quiet
only coming clean
what does not kill makes one wish it had

Waxwing

Spend your time in, the sky bleeds goodnight; the touch of two palms together turns the clouds inside out. So soft, so soft it goes, the trepid bridge we cross, it moans, we sway with the rhythm of the river, so that it splinters in two from the burden we brought. You have been defined. A sordid so and so, slipping through paper walls to seek out the hands of a clock; you'll set it back a minute and explain why in vowels. I wash my hands of all this, and water soaks and drips from the walls as my silent sigh trembles and shakes these limbs dry. I'm one for taking it hard, I'm one to worry about, I'll ask for regrets and stories unclouded by doubt. We'll sit watching quietly. We'll plead for the sun not to come, as we take the long way around our problems and drown them in smoke and bones. I hear that winter is here and I lock the doors, afraid of the loneliness that is the frozen contort of a land lost in a grey storm, a dead home. Too soon it seems, leaves swept from the streets, drown the sheen of snow melted from the march of feet.

Black Mirror

Will not wants wail when needed, bleeding slow
along long laments, howling wild now, in
lanterns, above the whispering night lights warm,
deep bronze, but sometimes tawny when the
fog bends, magnifying mists journeyed, brooding,
downcast thick little atmosphere, shuddering
hollow cloud, round out, wound down, holy world, whole
whirl, air admitted, sweet like love, flowers blooming,
cherry blossom, lofty ghosts lonesome in the hall when
my room is locked tight, silent in the blight, where,
waiting in vain, hearts will beat fast and then not at all.

Dear Lonely Life,

calling for someone who knows the ins and outs
of city sewers in winter mornings, know the
way to underground Shambhalah but get lost
in the forlorn dark, lonely see, a solid thing, one to
go missing with. Laying breadcrumbs to feed
senseless beasts, map a new way home. Scratch names in
the guardrails of the freeway around the city, leave street
names in love songs on the radio, write the way in riddles
to find where.

Love Translated Waves

about the old days,
"We went through a forest turning to flames,
burning up the sea, in hue the leaves grew hot, fell
free from branches twisted wide and reaching
to hold up the clouds, become the mast, steady,
a fragile embrace of waves, sweet breath of winter sifted
sank sails along curve of crescent moon, and
wind gathered, tide was a thing to forget,
knew not what sought, only that were
looking, little and lost, became a storm over a calm sea,
a wisp, an effervescence, as the wreck – splinter,
abandoned by the mast and the bow, churned by
a terrible sway, amen, amen, oh help
lord, oh save souls."

Willful

When I was young I used to pray for the rain,
but realized that god doesn't work that way and so
stole every last drop from heaven and prayed
for forgiveness, left them out to dry on the black
pitch; the day slow towed them away, and could not help
but hold my arms out, palms down to catch passing,
spirit's unhurried amalgamation in the sky. Closing
hands into a hollow fist, I whispered names across the
space, and they echoed in the distance between identities
tight printed in lines prescribing destiny and devotion to
a faraway star.

I never felt the pull of celestial bodies
They never told me of what I should dream
the most I could hear was that I was bad and broken
something unclean to be washed away in flames

so what if I'm the only one made of matter
and nothing else makes sense except in my mind
could there really be a watchdog we're warned of
could we be on our own, blind wandering

PART IV:
Trepidations

Brown Recluse

Mottled, sun spotted, mutt blood, blind,
the webbing between feelers crack, smoke damaged,
fibers thin and ill, slender wrists pop as they twist,
sending panic through disjointed limbs that
lose heat at first winter's flake, burrow fervently, invisible
but not always, the shaking is violent
when fight and flight chemicals drown perception,
encompassed, terror consumed unwillingly,
impelled gluttony, muculent palms, labored lungs, wide
eyed, dead amygdale, desiccated, an uncomfortable soul
encased in bones hollowed and cold.

Weary Woe'd

"with varying degrees of comprehensibility."

It is a condition that subsists
Old man syndrome
Heavy hag ridden

1956 beat poet recycled soul
Fell dead as Ginsberg howled
Thetan impels asiatic husk

Resigned ley lines
Towing aged dusk, grime
Everlasting Somniloquy

Stoned blown on one's own
Weeping Long Dawn
Tired Two-Bones

Mundane Malady
Soft Shelled
Walkabout Warbler

Locktender

to take in and fend
let the spent be steady
taut against debt
sure The Self is heavy lent
to match the mend
key keeper fumbling hands
crash and tremble without sound
send down
the motion is fixed
wholly out of bounds

I can't sustain the light sip
all bodies ferment

All Observer

Half of the last left
the back of my throat is tendered coal
loaned from paper fire
handed out in droves

taken aback for the sake of taking
and when the earth turns it low moans
so we won't feel it
drown in its motion or go down in its drone

the ship sailed the other day
amidst the late morning haze
to a shore we can't see
or choose to believe

free the frost
in staggered gasps
in belated winter
when it should be spring

Donner Party

I have to curtail this appetite
drunk on tepid night
horse fly holds under white steel awning
moon has taken to its woes
breathing out to breathe in smoke
so the note holds
or the end comes slow
but sure

build me a fire to be warm for the night
set me on fire to be warm the rest of my life

Ian Cook

Breaking Snake's Tooth to Make Good News

few that knew clouded out by noon
broached and taken note
took hold
in hands
take stock
flocked hoards

nocturnal in the daytime
mouth out the last rhyme
threaded ley lines
through flight of light

in the high wound come down
the take home is fair bound
in the quiet throng of knowing now
patient silence is common ground
begging in the rain for a name or a fate to tame
the synchophony in this white birdcage

Pluto

Oh god I am such a sad sap
taking back wishes from the well

and though the air is still
it is something not to trust

timid when the tongue is stuck
language is a long road

a holy home boarded
it's an effort to stay.

In a one place race
lengthy laps made me last

tending a mind made
motion mislaid and tame

shoddy frame is frail
sorry is a bad spell

careful feet compelled me
you made no moves.

Ian Cook

Martial Arts

the tremor of limber parts
enough to stay the bite
of ball and powder
swift turning in the palm
swayed west to east to rest
in Bodhi tree – broad trunk
to sprout in a hundred years

the martial arts won't stop a bullet
flesh bends in
hollow bones break
the body gone forever
the body gone to shade
the body gone forever
the body up in flames

Satiation

I've got my teeth in the grooves
biting hard to break pressure
the burden before us makes bad blood

bury to the neck
should the last lungs be filled until —
a still body breathes

I'll back up slowly into the night
wide eyed
lighting fires
along the black road

you are bad blood
you are the broken sound
that stops along world's curve

I don't know you at all and I miss you
let me be
taken care of

China Shop Ox

no longer looking for the hard won
so-sometimes come by
guiding with a blind eye
taking time to walk backwards

hard tunneled vision
in bad basic ways

arms up from side
palms down
see them steady
see how honest a man

tired and tried
refused to ask for direction

stumbling every step
fingers long counted regrets
moved on
to keeping track of bones

to get her

I had to piece it back together

replacing every part not made to love

King Vowel

marched mouth
ferried in
to tend the subtle wind
or keep the center cleared for fending

when bottom break takes way
maintain thin frame
distend

resign inside
embrace the bends
spread limbs wild

Hold back the breath a while

Summer Baby

my Summer Baby is a bright dawn
following the late winter, lazy rain

Summer Baby closed in quick
whispering by neck
pulls like a long tide

world wanderers
fettered to its turning
raised to yearn knowing

so recognized each other
reacquainted in the warm night
over smoke, stone

if she had no one she would have me
a place to rest and sleep

a claimed star
a named coast
a tame ghost
and she'll stay

I fall harder for it

Summer Baby came from the blind side
made heart tremor wild
placed stake upon time

Summer Baby sings her blues
lonesome down south

sitting in her arms
feels like I've come home
such familiar bones

tender touch is a loving stroke

if I break from this gravity
what will become of me

72's

Weary hands form a habit, holding patterns arthritic
in the grasp between two fingers
we spoke in tongues,
stacking holy verses,
unearthed voices,
dressed in all black as the wind lets up

These whispers are quiet angels of God.
They take – take
your time

What's Yours is Owl's

there's a black hole inside every body
here's a white lie tipping the tongue
like some sung mourning
motion in disdain is tame made
the space abound abhors the sound
my hands are a hound
my teeth maul
mark the earth
ghost of an herb
all vicarious borrowed bliss

Grace Kelly
I thought my bones were ready
for every word
to ruin me

I'm steady,
knew it was regretted,
never needed
a reason

What a world, what a world

Hog Branch

stowed away for steady blows
traipsing tight rope
with bones back stacked
swallow slow
keep a cold mouth closed

if you can fit hands
in my pockets
fold against fingers
leave them full

if the pull of pallid grip makes for mixed momentum
let everything go
make for the long way home

Old Void

two tone ghost moans escape the throat
and ghosts are always alone
the devil is always home
believe in means to make palms bleed, open to
catch the rain
be serene and borrow names muttered aloud in the dark

lost solitude of dimmed starlight
hampered by intrusive monument's glow; stark
and voracious
tide wise, collection in moon's phase
time hasty taken; opaque hourglass
slow self immolation over years
wary learning
hard lessons taught in blackout hours
time spent silent in smoke

moored upon furrow
spoke slake jawed and readymade and troubled
teethed and torn when picking roads in the dark
more so hopeless
how woeful is the waking night

Ian Cook

Conjugal

I am a lonely lamb,
a disenchanted man,
mute because of the hex on my voice,
song-singer made sinewy,
speech all cracked,
speaking quickly with fingers,
punctuation actuated upon my chest,
hold rot in hand,
where a new flower blooms,
once every afternoon,
it reeks of sorrow as it blossoms
fades and forms the moon,
dead petals given back to the earth,
and from the soot, the soil, comes a hurt,
sharp and short but deeply scarring,
like love unwound and then bound,
black holes in a kindness that is cracking,
stolen murmurs from a mouth rehearsed,
borrowed faithful words are lacking
any sort of regret to hope,
or could it be that we're all done mapping
the lines upon which we worship the most,
they led us home in the night,
calling us to cull the dulled senses from our bones,
dissected in parts and studied for wants,
anatomy of our mortal coil,
understanding of our foreign soul,
sutures set in,
fashioned from a languid thought,
they will keep my limbs together,

I did them myself,
I did myself in,
happiness is sin

Corpse Walker

A host upon a dozen bones
impelled against slow moaning orbit
following close script, hollow notation
setting stage to mimic old motions
or stay a stolid bust, eyes open without the iris

Life is much too long

Swapping masks in the dark
to learn how to mouth vowels
in steady wind, like larks
palm bearers, traced lines set in through top skin
fate decided – rehearsed and acted

a want to be a ghost again
to feel the tendrils of man purposed
hold and haul

instead

Suspended animation, only apparition
like the lonely moon trailing the day, the setting sun

Old Man Mars

on all groveling fours
scratching stone for some fire
slow beating chest to start a pulse
making a fist to make a point
hard hunch back with palms flat on the ground
pushes through the earth to make caves deep down
waiting for a spark to consume the dry tinder draped
welcoming a hot word and heavy stare
to bare knuckle
and downward tumble

praying to a faraway star
whose light is already burnt out

Ian Cook

Ghostwriting Suicide Notes

desperate modes condone forlorn mornings
singing two notes that turn to a long loony moan
inside lungs we swim
ready to be the song in the wind

the price of becoming something is:
being prone and steady.

fleet feet are restless but settle in the air
in tandem
read lips out loud so we are mouthing the same words
guess the language, pretend to understand

sitting tight with the shakes
limber—languid—statue state
motionless until request and upon being pressed
everything is flight, or fight, or alright with me
decisions are made hastily or not at all
never addressed
down around the bottom bones
enclosed in solid stones
leafless torn bark
needlessly worn to parts
in the deep dark

slowly go into the night

Morning Monsoon

I can't sleep because when I dream see everything
I've tried and what I'm supposed to be
on time and in line for the want to become habit, like being
familiar with failure

so still restless in the night
while time whistles away
blown out pillars of heat,
tempered and stoked in this hollow pit

wait for the waking world to bound down
to free the least inside of me that makes for less feeling
the steady carving of the far bank

I'm sure the weight of being born again will set me free
in a new body, be a better passenger, notes in hand
the cure is in the movement, steady and fluid

I'm sure enough with distance to amble on
and leave complimentary, when I go West to unsettle
the dust in these bones

Transmigration

Believe me I've got schemes and believe that I had
all the time in the world to wander the wondrous lone-
some as a man in the mirror who won't stop talking to
himself about himself in the dim light, stolid and atoned
by bones of solid stone homes hewn in the holy late night,
past
the constancy of morning's knowing nod, across the cool
grey wakeup call sung by lullaby birds to no one in the
dawn when I would try to fly and it happened once,
whereupon I was born.

PART V:
Family Matters

No More Rotten Son

I'm waiting for the right time to get my life together,
it's like waiting for the rain; I don't know what I want
but I need something that's been lost,
a ghost, she sings like meadowlarks,
I woke her from her sleep,
shaking Christmas bells in a clenched fist,
to pass the time whispering secret things,
like why everything isn't right,
and how can I be the good one,
no rotten son
no more

Equal Parts

She asked what my blood is like

I told her my mother was born in a city
swallowed by the Pacific
drowning in its own smog

I told her "my father is a pale conqueror crossing coasts"
hunting for thick pitch beneath the crust of the earth
tapping the surface with ear to the ground

I told her I was carefully constructed in equal parts

I stole the height of white fathers before me,
became lithe, sinewy
after patient gestation, tempered time spent
defying gravity
digging through open waters, bottomless pools
where lungs learned to stay full

I adorned the pigment of yellow mothers before me,
became tawny, fashioned a crown of ink
sat bowlegged beneath Boddhi tree to be silent
and count the passerby
scrawling rambling forms upon the canvas that lines
the inside of the mind

She said I had the right amount of Asian in me
I grabbed the corners of my eyes and pulled them back
towards her
and everything else
I have gone – passed and noted.

RPC

Tired father lay down, settle heat.
Fed up father open your hands, settle heat.
Go slow when patience won't go slow,
through the rafters a fragile wind chime, loose lip.
Long lay'n melancholy.

Weary father set down, unfurled, stretched across
the lips of a fire that whispers, hushes, gently,
and in the flame, gently
spoken an ounce of the fear we were,
was to be.

King Spider

stoke fires with your father's bones at night
keep it down and riled when turmoil is fresh inside
keeps close tired arms after morning flight

holding someone's head down
baptized in the wishing well
quench deep thirst swallowing spare change

miracles are manmade
poorly laid plans are often the blame
rotten hope is raised and tended with unsteady hand
clasping clamoring uncertainty and when I ask the wind
my name it replies in a whisper
then goes hush

and the world is solid and hollow
and old crow moans
until the bottom strung lungs become blood
and exhale is thick mist

our fingers are numb but still searching for a pulse

Tiger Glass

I think I'm haunted and my mother would know,
she's been following spirits

getting high before church on a Saturday afternoon
I've got bad ghosts and the smoke keeps them

and afterward read books without paying for them
we go to church early so there's more time to pray

Oath-Maker

Solvent in motion,
Saying you won't when you will,
Tip toe and still trip,
Prepare a silent retreat and remain tethered upon
the expanses of an all-seeing eye,
A question that is the answer,
Begged only by moving the lips further apart,
"Sorry"
All in parts, nodding and muttering sorry,
Fire burns in my mouth and I smother it with smoke,
I choke and I choke,
I choke and I choke

Black Francis

Old Buddha sticker faded, only "faith" left,
a form remains
oils from the palms of my hands,
sweat from tepid fingers,

"Been rubbing a bad charm with holy fingers"

Sallow contrails painted the setting sun,
finding familiar faces
in the grooves of grandmother's hands,
they cradle her husband forgetting her name

Ian Cook

Dear Alva Dean

Words form a memory, he picks at scabs on his neck and
the edges of his scalp,
bleed a little, let go a little,
to hear his history but not remember,
to hold his shoulders and feel him move like a wave
against the rocks – a stupor, violent.
I want to hear his stories but he doesn't know them,
only lived them.
Thin fingers, ethereal pluck the wiring of his brain,
sounding minor chords, shaking the dust off.
He says a kind word, becoming a whisper and a whimper.
He's told me the world in one-lines, love stories.
Sings boisterous, bass, full of belief
I still have to look for him when he loses himself.

Let the Skeleton Live

Unconcerned because temperance and time are short
a lake never let up
unbecoming of the land
hold up from the hip, the pace is long
ghost family made a trip to see home
a young son made the way on bones
stress tested on the lonely road
a regardless effort
ganged upon
atoned

I'll never forget the day my father said
that he was the loneliest man in the world

Ian Cook

A Wake

"every living creature on earth dies alone"

we hear everything around us die, but to us
it is only the wind
restless chattering in the day
enraptured branches in the night

like crows surrounding a black corpse
laying leaves and thin sticks, adornment
studying the wounds
remembering swirls in its obscure eyes
its feathers

like elephants left by mother's side for days
and then weeks and then they curl
becoming a corpse beside a corpse
passerby stops to stroke stranger's bones

like great apes congregate to watch
a cadaver carried out
refuse meals
and mope
and carry a corpse for days
rage against the body of the dead

Like cats coaxing old paths through the house
a constant calling out for what is not there
forgetting how to take care of itself

Tawny

I can be woe as me
blind around the seams
long hands
small plans
mother's wrists
father's heavy heart
looking for a start

Drained ebbed and flowed
so we can know
a thousand days at a time
to learn secret rhymes

Blind in light
memorizing words mouthed silent and alone
can't seem so right
memorizing thoughts bought and stoned
apropos so what
solitary haunts for homes

I can't stand in an empty room for long
without listening to the bones

Ian Cook

Sirens Last Night, and Tonight Too

still ilk
adolescent tense
present and blessed
the continent depressed

prairie boy plump fed petro-dollars
finding wives that only heard english
in television static
replicate the sounds, missing consonants
too many vowels too close together
my parents are alone together
language painted with gutter flush
mouth breather vocabulary
the beginnings of words tied to the ends of others
they forget to breath
accuse the other of respiratory thievery
"don't waste my air"

i once forgot that things could be haunted
wore the blanket my grandmother died in
and she became my skin
turning it grey and cold
a huddled mutt to be consoled
my mother said when you dream of loose teeth
you're losing family
and when my mother passes on lonesome
i'm a solitary son
i wonder how haunted an ambulance can become

my father was raised here, migrated from the wayward
west for central quiet plains, for grain
oceans swaying the rhythm of the wind,

water towers collapse under a cloudless vista, cleared of
contrails, an emptied sky, all birds grounded, the earth
warmed in the absence of atmosphere,
and Kansas was kindled fever void, voracious, volatile
endless space, where the coast will never be seen except
from the ceiling of the vault of heaven, where the land
is lucid, self-evident, unmistakable as the center
of disjointed lands, where woes concentrate themselves,
congregating miles above an old barren sea

PART VI:
Apparition and Old Ghost

No Really, Ghosts

my mother reminds us that all the world is haunted

there are good ghosts and bad ghosts and it is just chance
They sense you like a sifter moving through sand to find
shimmers breaking apart the sun smiling down

They find you as the swallow finds home, whistling
in the wind,
and when they catch song, swift sang back
on a better breeze, their direction is steadfast

They know you like old words
recited and written differently,
hastily played Chinese Whispers, quiet-like,
secretly in the dark

I hear their hello grow soft down the hallway —
Syncopated
to their own beat.

Ian Cook

Rectitude

She sang hallelujah as she inhaled
the smoldering sun
and became a hallowed mother
you can see her insides glow with the embers of the noon

My limbs are weary when we're done
pounding fists into stone
we'll mend it all

Crow Bone Crown

Batten down
worn out sound
air is inflexible mass
cornered
barred in
steady pace made to last
trepid jaw gnaws skin clean
ivory sings in heat's gleam
held back morning's fleet-footed leave
maintain missed memory
sea lost walkabout
get the bends, down
settle crown
full of hell
coming up
making moves wound
speak blood
croon old tunes
staking for the blame
keep the solid frame
take
taste pain
hold hope
sustain maimed claims
remain the same
carry on

King Crow, oh, King Bones, oh

Church Burnings

Exhaustion of easy life
stifled from the loose leash
breaking promises, it makes mother shake her head
but she understands
she told me so
so I would know
I don't have to stop my bad habits
skin tight bare bones act
carbon custody
whiskey sigh
weaving tall tales in the low light, early morning
laying hard
bending in the black roof
take whatever talk is about and loud
gather it tight, wrapped tinder
whisper it back through the filter and smoke, out
into dim dawn.

Death, Dismemberment, and Loss of Sight

how to identify your worth under a tarp
comprehensive liability is the lock
little white slip lets me be saved foremost
safe embrace in the hefting arms of grace
when death moves slowly it broaches
how to apply yourself

to reap

Ian Cook

Fistful of Feathers

Skylark light, shine bright
take your sweet song

Raven's wing, soft king silent
rip a tune from my tongue

White Dove, sink the sun's flight
teach me sad songs

Sparrow, calm, long hallelujah
hallelujah from a psalm

Nocebo

"I will harm"

waste no food on the walking dead
hungry husks to hobble
gently afflicted
without
placing hands
old word
evil eye
gnarled limb
white wailing dune
torrid pigment derived from bone
tea leaves
smoke trails
sibilating

"you will die soon and there is nothing
anyone can do about it"

body gives into belief
belief gives:
bad blood
breaks bones

Lion God Barong

Roll over, holy scarlet hoister of light
Jubilate denizen amongst woven machinations
riding thick wind over black tides
Eyes ever orbed outward
Watchful Brother of the oldest father
singing a silent note through steadfast leer
Story Maker of the turmoiled crashing coast
Lost God of the most ghosts
cradles softly within maw's bottom jaw
the seawater swamp forests of elden Indonesia
He enunciates words with no sound
speaking the radiance of the sun in each syllable
as the Great Lion pardons the thoughtful thinker
murmuring familiar dreams he has yet to finish

Osage Holy Man

In response to *Architecture of Home*, Norman Akers, 2010

Medicine man drums thunder, holy apparatus,
deerskin stretched taut,
he has become the all blue cloudless sky, faded
as the plotted land he is scrawled upon.
Atop his turtle mount, it takes a step with each
change of the season,
his destination is the other side of creation, keeping time,
his rhythm wills the turning of the cosmos, churning the
spirits of old gods to mark luminous messengers on a
star's chart, to create legless sparrows flying around this
celestial form, swirling the terrible sublime
on a silent night.

He shapes the moon within his center, commanding
the tide with each breath
inwards – outwards.

Scopophobia

Sweet Jesus girl
wishing me well
"Jesus Christ loves you"
waltzing back alleys of 9th St.
for all hours
shy shoulders crouched
facing the sides of houses
lost stop thoughts
before deciding a better way to wander
sneaking up in the night saying
"God bless you, God, Jesus loves you"
and not knowing who said it
I believed God stood at my back
willed me wanting with a soundless prayer
her breath; the soft steady confirmation of scopophobia

I did not recognize her today
and when she called me God's child
I had not heard
and regardless stopped to listen to her holy cadence
bible verses from rote
side notes in the margins Jesus rote
nodding thanks I walked away without a word
and felt cold gold around my neck

later, in the car heading home I saw her behind
the neighbor's shed nitpicking at her blue jean
dress, slow step through the alley to face grey chain links,
then walk north, in pilgrimage
across the highway and the rest of Kansas

Ghost Ocean

i feel it back again
a spirit beckoning
the melody she weeps becomes the voice in my head

i am alone
sleeping on my mother's bones
until she decides to come home

Ian Cook

Death while standing

in despair about old life
tame a holy ghost
spread wide and fly mild
tend to not mind
take time like a fast tide
receive peace clean
spring sun and moon brine
biding mine for wanting what is not
hiding kind to make the mark stick
bury our dead seated

Coffin Position

Mother frets; my bed faces the doorway
says I am openly inviting Skipton into my room

> *impatient twenty-three year old stuck on Iowa st.*
> *in a heavy rush*
> *rode his motorcycle into oncoming traffic last year*
> *black tarp: a horizon crossing lanes*

air moves as a wall when a door has opened
a host of heavy hands lay down upon shoulders and back.
As I lose my head to silent sleep, from the closet door,
opened just an inch, Skipton mutters in,
"Ohm", and it echoes, becoming a chant
in the still space above my bed

shadows of fingers on the outside edge
of my stubborn window, glass void of night frost,
warmed by the heat of lingering grip. For days now
I've been looking to the left,
expecting a shade in the doorway, or fingers over
wooden edges, slowly closing the closet door

rustled from loose sleep, I thought a friend, coy and sneak-
ing, came into my room and displaced
pressure and placed hand on my ankle hanging the edge,
and gently pressed it down into the
mattress and with a startled twist I turned
and the room was empty and the door was shut,
Skipton, poor stuck soul, had snuck up on me as I napped
in the cool noon of late fall

He tries to get my attention when noise envelopes my ears,

"Hey" he whispers, "You listening?"
from the back, behind,
and chills sprint down the rivets of my curved spine

Abrahadabra

is the sound of:
ringing wind chime
will create as I speak
unturning line cuts the front door
most high holy ghost
secret serpent coiled in spring, whispers silent things
like who survives the lion hunt
fingers locked in forgotten sign language
winged globe, steady dissipation
a locket of burnt birch, warm in palm
carved haze of bone dust
something to believe in

Edom

He sits a silent cipher,
thumb heavy, a pearl of hashish sat smoking on its tip.
He sips the light of the stone and becomes
a holy mountain,

a proverb mentioning the middle and the end
of dear creation etched in the feathers of a white
eye, counts the days with teeth of leviathan,
long sinewy things, they chatter together,
spelling new words for an old language, throat is
the skin of the land, a coarse road drawn by all the horses
of time, and as He speaks, stars flicker
and close their eyes in the night sky; cold wax
cakes the candle, drowning the wick in a thick malaise.

King Carrion

give me my antlers and I'll give up my ghost
bare bones
strip skin, little teeth
open up and
have a mess to clean

my mind is a crowed moon
waning in the day

separation of a:

> moth in flight
> smoke trail
> endless inhale

summer's end hosts:
cloud columns at night
head bowed in tempest
take rest when steady motions set
forms
made peace
maintained

often erroneous still frame
maimed and blamed
a body to make the motions mend
living in
a body haunted
with the ghost, hope
motley mourning wanes

A house of birds is my name
taking wings to make me tame

Hermes (Swift Mercury)

Oh eloquence, be my pattern.

The rhythm of communication is a cadence; birdsongs
from the branch winged warble.

Keeper of Boundaries, bringing word from and to:
the upper worlds, their lower companions.
Protector of Heralds, with a message divine,
travelers breaching porous barriers;
Go-between. Thieves and orators alike, wit in and around.

Swift Psychopomp take my ghosts, show them
the roads between. Come across a wayside marker,
a pile of stones set low, each passerby adds to the pile,
communion
through time, with consideration of space,
the border made // then crossed.

Conductor of Dreams, play them sweetly,
persuasion and special pleading. Taking in
the night, these thieving gifts are sacrificed to up
above, so it is right. Mediator, guide inner journeys,
and healing arts come from synchronicity, in self,
through—for self
sympathetic magic.

Seek and be sought, by winged feet.

ABOUT THE AUTHOR

At his core, Ian Cook is a mutt. An amalgamation of many things – different races, Swedish/German patronage, Chinese-Indonesian matronage, raised internationally. An in-between, a hybrid being, flowing, swimming, a life in and out of water, amphibious. He is a collection of multitudes, many selves, many-masks, anxiety, de-pression, bipolar disorder, sleeplessness, and dreams that don't end. He receives waves, whispers, and frequencies from beyond and translates them into Art, Music, and Poetry. Ian Cook is the author of Vishuddha, a collection of poems that deal with communication, what it is, and how the individual does it: by speaking, singing, screaming, writing, drawing, expressing, playing, by communing with All. He has had work featured in online and print journals such as Snarl Journal, KU's Kiosk Magazine, Avatar Review, and others. Ian lives in Lawrence, Kansas, with his partner Maddie, pups Mildred, and Cordelia, and rats Remy, and Grandpa.

We hope you enjoyed reading Ian Cook's "VISHUDDHA" Please order additional print copies from https://anamcara-press.com/ or from your favorite bookseller and leave a review for Ian Cook on your favorite bookseller's website!

OTHER BOOKS TO ENJOY FROM ANAMCARA PRESS

ISBN: 9781941237-08-3
$14.99

ISBN: 9781941237-33-5
$18.99

ISBN: 9781941237-30-4
$18.99

ISBN: 9781941237-13-7
$12.99

ISBN: 9781941237-18-2
29.99

ISBN: 9781941237-14-4
$14.99

Available wherever books are sold or at:
https://anamcara-press.com/

Thank you for being a reader! Anamcara Press publishes select works and brings writers & artists together in collaborations in order to serve community and the planet. *Your comments are always welcome!*

www.ingramcontent.com/pod-product-compliance
Lightning Source LLC
Chambersburg PA
CBHW071011120626
46546CB00003B/1042